Tana Hoban
DIG, DRILL, DUMP, FILL

Greenwillow Books

A DIVISION OF WILLIAM MORROW & COMPANY, INC.
NEW YORK

20 19 18 17 16 15 14 13 12 11 10

LIBRARY OF CONGRESS CATALOGING IN PUBLICATION DATA

Hoban, Tana. Dig, drill, dump, fill.
    Summary: Introduces, through photographs alone, heavy construction
machines: earth movers, mixers, diggers, and others.
    1. Earthmoving machinery—Pictorial works—Juvenile literature.
2. Construction equipment—Pictorial works—Juvenile literature.
[1. Earthmoving machinery—Pictorial works. 2. Construction
equipment—Pictorial works. 3. Machinery—Pictorial works]
I. Title.   TA725.H62   624′.152   75-11987
ISBN 0-688-80016-5   ISBN 0-688-84016-7 lib. bdg.

For my sister Freeda

What They Are and What They Do

Many machines get their names from what they do:
a roller rolls, a loader loads, and a dump truck dumps.
Some machines move on rubber tires and go where the
ground is hard or smooth. Some machines move on crawlers
and go where the ground is soft or bumpy.

⌃ **Crawler
hydraulic
backhoe** digs
large ditches
and cellars.

⌃ **Crawler front-end
loader** scoops and
loads rubble and
materials to be
hauled away. Also
digs large holes.

⌃**Paving breaker** cuts,
cracks, and crumbles
worn-out pavements
and streets for
repaving.

⌃ **Rubber-tired
backhoe and loader**
digs small ditches
and cellars.

Dump truck hauls and dumps earth, sand, gravel, and rocks.

Concrete truck mixes and hauls concrete.

Crawler crane with clamshell bucket scoops and loads gravel and other materials, digs deep holes, and bites into old buildings for demolition.

Small loader works in tight, small places where a big loader cannot fit. Scoops and unloads.

▲ **Rubber-tired front-end loader** digs and levels gravel, sand, and earth.

▲ **Roller** flattens and smooths fresh asphalt.

▲ **Crawler crane with electric magnet** lifts, sorts, loads, and moves metal.

▲**Trash truck** compresses trash and garbage and hauls it away.

▲**Street flusher** floods and washes the streets with water.